Sort It by TEXTURE

By Nicholas O'Hara

Gareth Stevens
PUBLISHING

first concepts

Sorting is putting things that are alike together. You can sort by how things feel to touch.

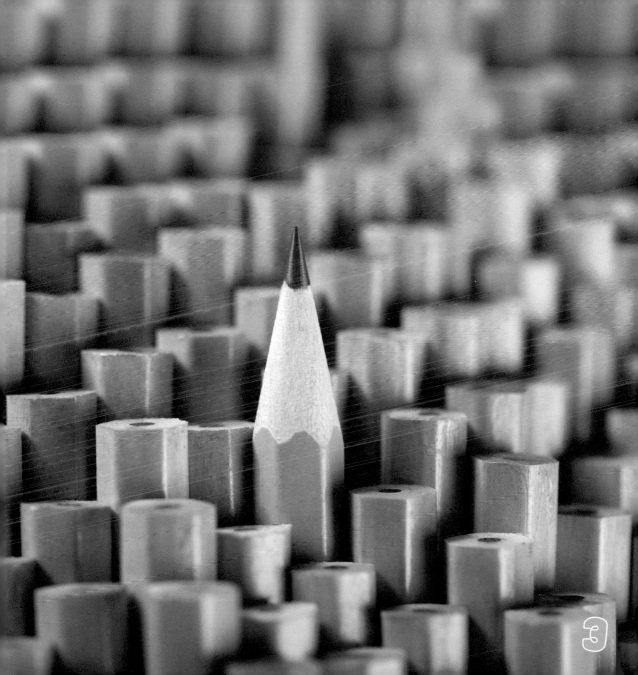

Wood can feel
smooth or rough.

This wood feels rough.

Rocks can feel smooth
or rough.

These rocks
feel smooth.

Toys can feel hard
or soft.

These toys feel soft.

Hats can feel hard
or soft.

These hats feel hard.

Skin can feel bumpy
or smooth.

This skin feels bumpy.

13

Roads can feel
bumpy or smooth.

This road
feels smooth.

Fruit can feel bumpy
or smooth.

This fruit feels bumpy.

Treats can feel sticky
or dry.

These treats
feel sticky.

Pasta can feel dry
and hard or wet
and slippery.

This pasta feels wet
and slippery.

How do you think
each of these animals
would feel?

23

Please visit our website, www.garethstevens.com. For a free color catalog of all our high-quality books, call toll free 1-800-542-2595 or fax 1-877-542-2596.

Cataloging-in-Publication Data

O'Hara, Nicholas.
Sort it by texture / by Nicholas O'Hara.
p. cm. — (Sort It out!)
Includes index.
ISBN 978-1-4824-2581-9 (pbk.)
ISBN 978-1-4824-2582-6 (6 pack)
ISBN 978-1-4824-2583-3 (library binding)
1. Materials — Texture — Juvenile literature. I. O'Hara, Nicholas. II. Title.
TA418.7 O43 2016
620.1'1292—d23

First Edition

Published in 2016 by
Gareth Stevens Publishing
111 East 14th Street, Suite 349
New York, NY 10003

Designer: Sarah Liddell
Editor: Therese Shea

Photo credits: Cover, p. 1 (polka dots) Victoria Kalinina/Shutterstock.com; cover, p. 1 (fruit) Valentyn Volkov/Shutterstock.com; p. 3 Stocksnapper/Shutterstock.com; p. 4 (left) Evlakhov Valeriy/Shutterstock.com; p. 4 (right) PhotographyByMK/Shutterstock.com; p. 5 Opas Chotiphantawanon/Shutterstock.com; p. 6 Perfkos/Shutterstock.com; p. 7 Apollofoto/Shutterstock.com; p. 8 Poznyakov/Shutterstock.com; p. 9 MAii Thitikorn/Shutterstock.com; p. 10 (left) Alex Staroseltsev/Shutterstock.com; p. 10 (right) Lucy Liu/Shutterstock.com; p. 11 stockphoto mania/Shutterstock.com; p. 12 (elephant trunk) Aaron Amat/Shutterstock.com; p. 12 (hand) Antonio Guillem/Shutterstock.com; p. 13 Anan Kaewkhammul/Shutterstock.com; p. 14 AlexanderZam/Shutterstock.com; p. 15 Twenty20 Inc/Shutterstock.com; p. 16 margouillat/Shutterstock.com; p. 17 Viktar Malyshchyts/Shutterstock.com; p. 18 (marshmallows) Texturis/Shutterstock.com; pp. 18 (candy), 21 Africa Studio/Shutterstock.com; p. 19 de2marco/Shutterstock.com; p. 20 (left) nelik/Shutterstock.com; p. 20 (right) motorolka/Shutterstock.com; p. 23 (main) Eric Isselee/Shutterstock.com; p. 23 (turtle) Zorandim/Shutterstock.com.

Printed in the United States of America

CPSIA compliance information: Batch #CS15GS: For further information contact Gareth Stevens, New York, New York at 1-800-542-2595.

3 1333 04474 8455